Ware has had a reputation for good food for almost as long as St. Mary's Parish Church. In 1400, Chaucer said of the cook in *The Canterbury Tales* that he could roast, and boil, and broil and fry, make thick soup and well bake a pie". The cook's name was Roger Hogg of Ware, and scholars think that he was named after a real person. The reason the town stood so high in the hospitality stakes was that it was a major stopping point on the Old North Road – the main route from London to York and Scotland. The south side of the High Street, known as Water Row, was a continuous line of coaching inns. Kings, foreign princes, nobles of church and state all stayed in these inns. In 1539, the Countess of Rutland and her retinue stayed at a Ware inn and consumed beef, mutton, lamb, chicken and five rabbits as well as the delicacies of calves' feet and crayfish for breakfast the next day. But Ware was also famous for the malt it made for the brewing industry so the countess's party drank a 'kylderkyne' of ale (about 18 gallons), "a single beer for my Lady", a pint of white wine, a bottle of claret and a pint of sack. Many of these visitors were pilgrims on their way to the Shrine of Our Lady at Walsingham in Norfolk and there was a special altar in St. Mary's where pilgrims could pray.

When pilgrimages were banned by Henry VIII, the inns suffered accordingly. It is thought that the Great Bed of Ware – a very large oak four-poster, now in the Victoria & Albert Museum – was made as a way of attracting visitors. A German prince first described it in the White Hart Inn. A little later in 1601 Shakespeare included it in *Twelfth Night*, but his brief mention was nothing compared to the play, *Northward Ho*, by Thomas Dekker and John Webster, which is set wholly in Ware. Apart from references to the Great Bed, the play's main interest – not surprisingly – is in food including crayfish, spitchcocks and fat trout.

In more modern times the Market Place (the area, including the road, outside the Town Hall), was surrounded by inns. In 1906 the town had more licensed premises per head of population than any other district in Hertfordshire. There were 16 inns alone on the south side of the High Street. In the 1960's Ware led the way with good food. There were fish, meat and vegetable shops offering a full range of local and exotic delicacies. There was also a remarkable establishment called the Epicure Delicatessen. A butcher's shop occupied the Town Hall building in the early part of the 20th century, and its Christmas display of game, poultry and meat on the front of the shop reached to the first floor windows. It's nice to know that good food remains an important part of Ware's everyday life whether it is shops, restaurants, fast food or good old fish and chips.

The Oldest Building in Ware

You might think that St. Mary's Church has little to do with you. Well, you would be wrong. More than 23,000 Ware people will pass through the doors of the Church and its hall in an average year and less than a third of them are regular 'church-goers'. This book has been created to raise funds to ensure that the building continues to be enjoyed by Ware people in the years and indeed centuries to come. It is our duty and indeed privilege to make sure our children, their children and their children's children continue to have use of it.

The earliest documented evidence of a township of Ware is the Domesday Book, but there is a record of a Church presence as early as 1078. The present building, standing proud at the top of the High Street, is largely due to the generosity of Joan (the Fair Maid) of Kent, Princess of Wales and wife of the Black Prince. The majority of the Church dates from 1380.

The list of Clergy dates from the 11th century though records have been better kept since the Church became a Trinity College Cambridge 'living'. They own the title of land and right of presentation.

Contact with Trinity College remains a highly valued relationship almost five centuries later. And indeed in 2005 the College paid for the restoration of the chancel roof. As with the town the hospitality of the Parish Church, this first 'Staging Post' on the North Road has had a varied history, adapting to an ever-changing role. The building has hosted the town and its community in every aspect of life: the market place; the refuge in traumatic times; the concert and meeting hall; the focus of local authority and justice; the marker of rites of passage, birth, marriage, death. No accurate records tell us of numbers in antiquity, nor those resting within the body or grounds of the church, no records were required before the mid 16th century. The only certainty is that the Church continues – despite various states of collapse and failure, restoration and revival – spanning the centuries.

In modern times the Parish Church still serves as a centre and focus of Christian worship; the platform for performance of music and the arts; where people pass through and assemble in portals of antiquity still serving the community. Visitors come to soak in the architecture or historic monuments. Schools, both church and secular, visit to fulfil requirements of modern 'national curriculum demands' as well as cycles of yearly services. Mums bring toddlers to play, little ones learn about music, and friends come to gossip. Families come to sing carols at Christmas and to have a cup of tea at the annual bazaar. We warmly welcome those needing to be fed both spiritually and physically. We thank God for the continuing rich culture of hospitality and nourishment which this ancient town, and its people, offer.

Contents

Soups & Stuff

Butternut Squash & Ginger Soup

"This dish can be frozen for up to 2 months"

1 onion, chopped
1 leek, washed and diced
1oz butter
1 clove garlic, crushed
1 clove root ginger, grated
1 large butternut squash, peeled de-seeded and chopped
2 medium potatoes, peeled and chopped
2 teaspoons Marigold vegetable stock powder

Sweat the onion and leek in butter until soft but not coloured, add the garlic and ginger and cook for a minute. Add the squash and other ingredients together with 1 pint of water.

Cover and simmer for about 30 minutes until tender. Blend until smooth.

Serve with croutons.

Anne Lloyd-Skinner ———————————————— Serves 4

Tuna Quiche

"This can be good for lunch, a starter or a light supper"

225g wholemeal pastry
185g can of Tuna, drained
3 eggs
300g cottage cheese
50g grated cheese

Roll out pastry and line an 8" flan dish. Bake blind for 15 minutes at 180°C (fan oven).

Place flaked tuna in flan case.

Beat cottage cheese, eggs and grated cheese together and pour over tuna.

Bake for 25 minutes at 180°C (fan oven).

Tom Yum Kai

"This recipe is a classic Thai dish and the trick is not to cook it too long. The essence is to experience the flavours in full by using fresh ingredients. Cook for too long and the soup will become cloudy. The chicken can be substituted with 16-24 medium shrimps and the soup will be called Tom Yum Gong"

1 chicken breast, sliced into very small pieces
1-2 cans of straw mushrooms or 1 lb of small white mushrooms, halved
3-4 bottom halves of lemon grass stalks, quartered and crushed
6-8 Kaffir lime leaves, roughly shredded (use lime rinds as substitute)
2-3 fresh chillies, lightly crushed
400ml of good chicken or vegetable broth
Thai Fish Sauce or cooking salt
Juice of l lemon
Sprig of coriander, roughly chopped

Put all ingredients into a large saucepan and bring liquid to the boil. Skim the liquid to ensure that it remains clear.

Let the liquid simmer until the chicken is done, continuing to skim off any froth on top of the liquid. When the soup is ready add Thai fish sauce, which is very salty, to personal taste or add cooking salt. At the point of serving, stir in juice of one lemon and sprinkle with the coriander.

Serves 6

No. 1 Thai Café

1 West Street
Ware
Herts SG12 9EE
☎01920 485978

Opening times:
Monday to Saturday 9.30am - 2.30pm &
6.00pm - 9.30pm

A very pretty, tiny building bursting with
character.

Our customers tell us that we are the most
popular restaurant in town.

Thai cuisine is essentially a centuries old
marriage of Chinese and Indian influences
that blends harmoniously into something
uniquely Thai. This restaurant is also open
for a cup of coffee or the now famous
English breakfast, so loved by our customers.

Three Smoked Fish Pâté

"Ideal for a special occasion. Slice when well chilled, and serve with warm granary toast & butter. This recipe can be made with a food processor or by hand. This pâté can be frozen"

100g smoked salmon slices
175g smoked trout, skinned & boned
75g butter
75g cream cheese
Juice of ½ a lemon
Salt & Freshly ground black pepper

100g smoked salmon pieces, skinned & boned
50g butter
50g cream cheese
Juice of ½ a lemon
Salt & Freshly ground black pepper

175g smoked mackerel fillets, skinned and boned
75g butter
75g cream cheese
Juice of ½ a lemon
Salt & Freshly ground black pepper

Line a 2 pint terrine or loaf tin with cling film, and then line with the slices of smoked salmon.

For the trout pâté, put all the ingredients into a processor, and blend for a few moments until smooth. Turn into the prepared tin and level out evenly. Stand tin in the refrigerator while you prepare the next layer.

For the salmon pâté put all the ingredients into a processor (no need to wash bowl in-between) process until smooth. Carefully spread this mixture in a layer on top of the trout pate and return to refrigerator.

Repeat this process for the mackerel pâté and spread it on top of the salmon pâté. Wrap any surplus smoked salmon over the top of the terrine. Wrap with clingfilm up and over the top of the pâté and chill overnight before serving.

Sallie Klippel ———————————————— Serves 10

Griddled Scallops

"For a simple, yet delicious starter"

8 fresh scallops with orange roe
8 slices smoked pancetta
2 tablespoons fresh chopped parsley
Olive oil for brushing griddle and scallops
before cooking

Place each scallop on a slice of pancetta. Roll up and secure with wooden cocktail stick. Brush lightly with olive oil.

Heat griddle until very hot; place wrapped scallops on griddle; cook until bacon crisp – turn frequently.

Serve as a first course with wild rocket leaves, a slice of lemon and French bread.

Prawn Bisque

1.2kg uncooked prawns with shells on
150g carrots, peeled and diced in 2 cm lengths
300g onion, peeled and diced in 2 cm lengths
1 bayleaf
1 sprig of thyme
10g parsley stalks
50ml brandy
300ml dry white wine
150g long grain rice
1.5 litres fish stock
400ml double cream
250g unsalted butter
Cayenne pepper
Salt and freshly ground pepper

In a large saucepan cook the carrots, onion, parsley, thyme and bay leaf in 50g butter until they are light brown. Wash the prawns, then cook with the carrots and onions until the prawns turn pink. Season with 12g of salt and a little pepper. Sprinkle with the brandy and set alight. Add the wine and allow to cook gently until the mixture has reduced. Add 250ml of the fish stock and cook gently for 10 minutes.

In the meantime, cook the rice in 750ml of fish stock. Add the rice and its cooking liquid, together with the cooking liquid from the prawns. Liquidize everything until smooth. Pass through a fine sieve and dilute this purée with 500ml of fish stock. Bring to the boil, then pass through a fine sieve one more time.

To finish the soup add 200g of butter and 400 ml of double cream. Season to taste, adding a little cayenne pepper. To serve, dot with cream and a small sprig of dill.

Le Rendez-vous

64 High Street
Ware
Herts SG12 9DA
☎01920 461021
www.lerendez-vousrestaurant.co.uk

Opening times:
Tuesday - Sunday Lunch 12.00 – 3.00pm
Monday – Saturday Dinner 7.00 – 11.00pm

French modern cuisine. Jorge Noble is head chef running the kitchen. Lesley runs the front of house. Parties catered for, contact us for any special requirements.

The exposed brickwork and beams add to the atmosphere in this intimate, characterful, French restaurant. Using only high quality fresh seasonal products, with a contemporary approach to some traditional recipes and classic food combinations. An extensive wine list. Pretty enclosed terraced garden for al fresco dining in the summer months.

Avocado and Grapefruit Starter

"Refreshingly different"

2 large grapefruits
1 large (or 2 small) avocados
Small tub of single cream
Small tub of crème fraîche (full or half fat)
1 teaspoon of cayenne pepper
Sprinkle of paprika or a sprig of mint

Segment grapefruit and cut into bite size pieces – retain half shells (skins) if you wish to serve in them. Pat off any surplus juice from the segments with kitchen roll.

Cut avocado into bite size pieces. Combine fruits and place in a bowl. Mix the cream and crème fraîche together and add the cayenne pepper – add to the fruit, and carefully combine until all fruit is coated.

Pile the fruit mixture back into the half grapefruit shells and garnish with a sprinkle of paprika, and/or a sprig of mint.

Honey and Walnut Bruschetta

"This was served at The Beehive Pub near Ickworth and was wonderful with a glass of good red wine"

A French bread stick, sliced diagonally into 1"
slices
allow 2 pieces per person
4 x ¼" thick slices of goats' cheese
8 walnut halves
8 good teaspoons of clear honey
butter for spreading

Butter the slices of bread right to the edges.
Place the pieces of cheese in the centre of
the bread. Place the walnut halves in the
centre of the cheese. Dribble the honey over
the walnut and goats' cheese.

Pre-heat the grill until very hot – grill the
bread and cheese until the cheese starts to
melt, and the edges of the bread are golden
but not burned.

Serve with a few rocket leaves and drizzle
with olive oil and balsamic vinegar.

for John Budworth ———————————— **Serves 4   17**

Pizza Swirls

"This recipe can be made as a starter or for a picnic"

For the base
200g self-raising flour
50g margarine
50g grated cheese
6-8 tablespoons milk

For the filling
2 tablespoons tomato sauce and then
choose from this list:
100g Tuna
50g cheese
2 tablespoons sweetcorn
½ chopped onion

Sieve flour into the bowl. Cut up the margarine, add it to the bowl, and rub the flour and margarine together until the mixture looks like breadcrumbs. Add the grated cheese and the milk. Use a knife to bring the mixture together into a dough.

Prepare whichever filling you have chosen.

Knead the dough to make it smooth and then roll it out into a rectangle. Spread the filling over the dough and roll it up.
Cut the roll into slices 4cm thick.
Turn the rolls on their ends and arrange on a baking tray
Bake for 12-15 minutes and cool on a cooling tray.

Elissa Jones ———————————————— Serves 8

Baba Ghanoush

4 medium aubergines (800g)
1 lemon
1 garlic clove, crushed
6 tablespoons extra virgin olive oil
2 tablespoons chopped parsley
½ teaspoon ground cumin

Preheat oven to 190°C. Cut the aubergines lengthways and rub surfaces with a cut lemon. Slash with a knife and brush with 1 tablespoon of oil. Bake flesh side up for 45 - 50 min or until soft but not too brown. Remove and cool.

Scoop out flesh and whizz with other ingredients adding remaining olive oil a little at a time until it is of a 'dippable' consistency. Refrigerate.

Serve with warmed pitta bread and olives as a starter.

Anne Lloyd-Skinner ———————————— Serves 4   19

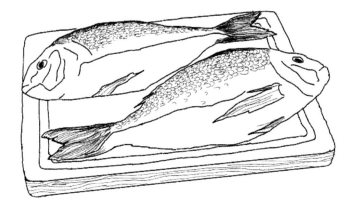

Fish

Crispy-crumbed Fish

50g fresh breadcrumbs
Small handful freshly chopped flat-leafed parsley
Zest of 1, and juice of ½, lemon
4 x 150g haddock or pollock fillets
½ teaspoon Dijon mustard

Preheat the oven to 180°C. Put the breadcrumbs into a bowl with the parsley, and lemon zest. Mix well, then set aside.

Put the fish fillets onto a baking tray. Mix the mustard and half the lemon juice in a bowl with a little sea salt and freshly ground black pepper, then spread over the top of each piece of fish. Spoon the breadcrumb mixture over the top. Don't worry if some falls off.

Cook in the oven for 10-15 minutes until the fish is cooked and the breadcrumbs are golden. Pour the remaining lemon juice over the top and serve.

Anne Lloyd Skinner ———————————— Serves 4

Smoked Haddock Crunch

1 lb smoked haddock
1 oz butter
2 oz plain flour
¼ pint evaporated milk
7 oz can sweetcorn
1 oz cheddar cheese, grated
1 packet crisps, crushed

Poach haddock with ¾ pint water, black pepper and ½ oz butter. Skin and flake. Spread sweetcorn over the fish.

Make up a white sauce with the butter, plain flour and milk.

Combine with the fish, sprinkle with crisps and cheese.

Bake for 15 minutes at 200°C in a gratin dish.

Prawns, Corn & Tomato in Spicy Coconut Sauce —

12 oz prawns (frozen and thawed)
8 oz can sweetcorn
4 large skinned & chopped tomatoes
2 dried chillies
1 chopped hard boiled egg
1 teaspoon brown sugar
3 oz desiccated coconut
2 teaspoons soy sauce
1 squeezed lemon
4 finely sliced spring onions

Season prawns with salt and pepper. Stir and leave to stand for at least 10 minutes.

Bring 14 fl oz water to the boil. Add ½ teaspoon salt and the corn, sugar and tomatoes. Cook gently for 3 minutes.

Crumble dried chillies add to the boiled egg and grind to a paste. Add to pan.

Sprinkle in coconut, stirring continuously. Reduce heat and simmer for 10 minutes. Add lemon and soy sauce to taste. Serve sprinkled with spring onions.

Serve with plain boiled basmatic rice

Anne Lloyd Skinner ———————————— Serves 4

Boozy Garlic Prawns

500g raw prawns, peeled and de-veined
50g butter
1 clove garlic, crushed
2 tablespoons chopped flat-leaved parsley
100ml dry sherry or dry white wine
Brown bread
Lemon wedges

Melt the butter in a small pan, add the garlic and fry gently for 1-2 minutes.

Add the prawns and cook for 2-3 minutes until pink all over.

Add the parsley and sherry and cook for a further minute.

Serve the prawns in the liquid and garnish with brown bread and lemon wedges.

Seafood Lasagne

500g cocktail prawns
250g small scallops
500g crab meat
3 cloves garlic, minced
2 pints double cream
1 glass dry white wine
2 boxes lasagne sheets
200g parmesan cheese, shaved

Cook lasagne sheets, according to label and allow to cool. Sweat the minced garlic in a saucepan, add the wine and let it simmer until the content is reduced by two thirds.

Slowly add the cream and continue to simmer until the mixture is a consistency which coats the back of a spoon. Take the sauce off the heat and stir in all the seafood. Season to taste

In a roasting pan, place a layer of cooked pasta then spoon over a layer of the seafood mix. Continue until all the ingredients have been used. Cover with foil and place in a pre-heated oven at 180°C for 45 minutes.

To serve, cut pieces from pan and sprinkle with the shaved parmesan. Garnish with rocket salad and lemon wedge.

Jacoby's Restaurant and Bar

Churchgate House
15 West Street
Ware
Herts SG12 9EE
☎01920 469181
www.jacobys.co.uk

Opening times:
Monday 7.00 – 9.30pm
Tuesday – Saturday 12.00 – 2.30pm
& 7.00 – 9.30pm

Set in the beautiful and historic
Churchgate House. The building
dates back to the 16th century. The menu changes regularly taking inspiration from home and around the world. Fresh produce is at the heart of the cooking, which has been described as classical in its preparation but with a modern twist.

Traditional Fish Pie

700g potatoes, peeled
2 large leeks, chopped
300ml vegetable water plus 2
tablespoons skimmed milk
1 tablespoon chopped fresh parsley
or chives, plus extra to garnish
25g polyunsaturated margarine
50g plain white flour
450g skinned and boned cod, cut
into chunks
100g frozen, peeled prawns,
defrosted
50g frozen peas, defrosted
Salt and freshly ground black
pepper

Cook the potatoes in boiling, lightly salted water until just tender. Meanwhile, cook the leeks in a small amount of lightly salted boiling water for about 5 mins. Drain them both well, reserving the cooking liquid.

Mash the potatoes, adding 2 tablespoons of milk. Make up the remaining 300ml with the cooking liquid from the potatoes and leeks. Add the chopped parsley or chives.

Put the margarine, flour and milk mixture into a saucepan. Heat, stirring constantly with a small wire whisk or wooden spoon, until thickened and smooth. Check the seasoning, adding salt and pepper if necessary. Pre-heat the oven to Gas Mark 5. Put the cod in the base of a 1.2 litre baking dish and scatter the cooked leeks, prawns and peas on top. Pour over the sauce. Pipe or spoon the mashed potato over the surface.

Bake for 30-35 minutes until cooked and browned. Serve sprinkled with more chopped parsley or chives.

Karol Bradbury ——————————————— Serves 4

1 lb fillet of salmon or salmon pieces, skin removed
100g basmatic rice, cooked
250g button mushrooms, roughly chopped
4 large spring onions, finely chopped
1 clove garlic, finely chopped
1 tablespoon olive oil
1 hard boiled egg, chopped
500g puff pastry
150g crème fraîche
2 tablespoons chopped parsley
2 tablespoons chopped chives
Salt and Pepper
1 egg to glaze pastry

Heat the olive oil in a frying pan and cook the onions, mushrooms and garlic with a pinch of salt. Cook over a low heat for about 10 minutes stirring occasionally. Set aside.

Divide the pastry into two. Roll out one half on a lightly floured surface 1" larger than the salmon fillet. Place the salmon in the centre of the pastry. Season. Lay the mushroom mixture on top of the salmon. On top of this add the cooked rice and then the chopped egg on top of the rice, spreading evenly.

Brush the pastry edge with a little milk. Roll out the remaining pastry and cover the fish with it. Press the edges to seal, trim off excess pastry and use a fork to bind the edges or flute it. Brush the whole thing with beaten egg. Bake in a pre-heated oven at 180°C for about 20 minutes until pastry is golden. Whilst the fish in the oven blend the crème fraîche with the chives. Serve with a green salad.

Green Fettucine with Salmon

"This recipe is very good with tuna instead of salmon"

1 oz butter
1 small onion, finely chopped
1 garlic clove, crushed
1 tablespoon tomato purée
Good pinch of cayenne pepper (optional)
7 fl oz medium or dry white wine
Salt and pepper
12 oz fettuccine verdi
5 fl oz single cream
7½ oz can red salmon, drained and flaked

Heat butter in frying pan and cook onion and garlic for 4-5 minutes until softened.
Add tomato purée, cayenne pepper, wine and seasoning. Simmer for 3-4 minutes or until reduced by half.

Meanwhile cook pasta in large pan of boiling salted water as directed on packet.

Add cream and salmon to onion mixture, bring to boil and simmer for 1-2 minutes.

Drain pasta well, return pan and toss in hot sauce. Serve with a green salad.

Pat Collin ————————————————————— Serves 4

Mayor's Paella

8 oz rice
4 chicken breasts
8 oz squid
4 oz mussels
4 oz chorizo
4 oz shelled prawns
4 oz diced peppers
4 oz peas
1½ pints chicken stock
Butter for cooking
Saffron
Turmeric
Cooking oil

Dice and fry chicken breasts and set aside. Fry rice until golden brown. Add chicken, squid, and prawns and cook thoroughly. Add peppers and peas. When cooked add stock with saffron infused in it. Add turmeric to colour.

Bring to the boil, then lower heat and simmer until liquid has evaporated.

Season with salt and pepper to taste.

Serve with a green salad.

Ligurian Fish Stew

4 sea bass or sea bream fillets, scaled & cut into strips
100g black olives
20 salted capers, rinsed
2 cloves of garlic, peeled & chopped
2 large shallots
1 handful of parsley
30g pine nuts
20g dried porcini mushrooms, soaked in hot water
4 washed salted anchovies
2 medium potatoes, peeled & cut into small pieces
30ml extra virgin olive oil
½ large glass of dry white wine
400g ripe, peeled, tomatoes or good quality tinned

Boil the potatoes until cooked, drain and reserve. Heat the oil in a large, deep frying pan. Melt the anchovies in the hot oil, add the shallots, garlic, capers & half of the chopped parsley. Heat everything for a couple of minutes without allowing the shallots to brown but just sweat down, then add the olives, pine nuts and re-hydrated porcini mushrooms with a little of the mushroom stock. Don't use it all and avoid the sediment!

Pour in the white wine and allow some to evaporate before adding the tomatoes. Allow to heat for a few minutes, breaking down the tomatoes with a wooden spoon as you go. Then add the pieces of boiled potato, stirring well. When some of the liquid has again evaporated, add the cut up fillets laying them flesh side down in the stew pushing them under the liquid to absorb the flavour.

Allow to cook for about 10-15 minutes on a low heat and cover if you do not want any further liquid to evaporate. Simply serve on its own, garnished with the other half of the parsley and a chunk of crusty bread!

Serves 2

Byron's Fine Food

68 High Street
Ware
Herts SG12 9DA
☎01920 460808
Email: byronsfinefood@aol.com

Opening Times:
Monday – Wednesday 9.30 – 5.00pm
Thursday 9.30 – 3.00pm early closing
Friday & Saturday 9.30 – 5.30pm

Byron's Fine Food was opened in August 2005 and has quickly established a business that is highly regarded locally. We have a strong bias towards home-made, local and regional produce and with a growing repertoire of recipes; we make a number of popular products in house. To complement this we also supply the best of the Mediterranean with a vast array of Italian and Spanish specialities plus a good selection of Eastern and Asian ingredients.

We offer a 10% discount to senior customers on Tuesday (males over 65/females over 60), and produce a 'Recipe of the Week' which is printed for customers to take away as inspiration.

Fancy Kedgeree

1 medium onion, sliced
1 green pepper, sliced
1 fennel bulb, sliced
8 medium mushrooms, thickly sliced
2 medium red chillies, de-seeded and finely chopped
2 smoked trout fillets - flaked
2 heaped tablespoons brown rice
2 dessertspoons raisins
2 dessertspoons frozen peas
1 tablespoon of olive oil

Cook the brown rice, according to instructions. Add the raisins and peas about 5 minutes from the end of cooking. Stir fry the vegetables in a wok or frying pan with the oil - about 10 minutes.

When cooked add the trout to the rice saucepan and let it stand for about 1 minute. Drain and mix the contents of the saucepan with the vegetables.

Serves 2

David's Fresh Tuna

2 medium tuna steaks
12 oz fresh tomatoes, skinned and chopped
(you can use tinned)
1 large onion, finely sliced
1 clove garlic, finely chopped
1 teaspoon dried or fresh mixed herbs
Olive oil to cook onion

Heat enough olive oil in a large thick-based saucepan or casserole dish. Fry onion until soft but not brown.

Place tomatoes on top of soft onion; heat gently until hot.
Place tuna steaks on top of onion mixture side by side; sprinkle on herbs.

Place lid on and cook gently for approximately 3 minutes and then turn tuna; cook for a further 3 minutes.

Serve with fresh green beans, new potatoes or egg noodles.

Cheese & Vegetables

Italian Flag Pasta

8 oz pasta
1 medium onion, finely chopped
1 red pepper
100g mangetout or sugar snap peas
2 tablespoons of pesto
Parmesan cheese to sprinkle

Cook the pasta in boiling water for 10 mins.

While pasta is cooking, fry onion until soft.
Add pepper and mangetout, and stir fry for
about 4 minutes.

When pasta is cooked, strain, return to the
saucepan and stir in the pesto. Combine all
the ingredients in the frying pan and serve
with grated parmesan and a green salad.

Serves 2

Vegetable Lasagne

1 tablespoon olive oil
1 medium onion, chopped
1 medium courgette, sliced
1 medium red and 1 yellow pepper
de-seeded and chopped
225g mushrooms, sliced
320g jar of tomato pasta sauce
1 teaspoon dried mixed Italian herbs
300ml skimmed milk
25g plain white flour
1 tablespoon polyunsaturated
margarine
50g extra-mature Cheddar cheese,
grated
125g no pre-cook lasagne sheets (6
sheets)
Salt and freshly ground black pepper

Preheat the oven to Gas Mark 5. Heat the oil in a large frying pan or wok and sauté the onion until softened (3-4 minutes). Add the courgette, peppers and mushrooms and stir fry for another 2 minutes or so. Tip in the pasta sauce and dried herbs and season with salt and pepper. Remove from heat.

Make the cheese sauce. Put the milk, flour and margarine in a medium saucepan. Bring to the boil, stirring constantly with a wire whisk, until the sauce blends and thickens. Add the cheese and cook gently for about 30 seconds. Stir until melted. Season to taste with salt and pepper.

Spoon half the vegetable mixture into an oblong ovenpoof dish and lay half the lasagne sheets on top. Spread 3-4 tablespoons of the cheese sauce over the pasta and then add the remaining vegetable mixture. Cover the rest of the sheets and spread the rest of the cheese sauce on top. Transfer to the oven and bake for 40-45 minutes until golden brown.

Stilton Cheesecake

"This can be made the day before, then warm through in a hot oven for 15-25 minutes on a baking sheet. It is not suitable for freezing"

For the base:
125g breadcrumbs
60g Parmesan cheese freshly grated
30g butter, melted
Salt and freshly ground black pepper

For the filling:
4 medium eggs,
200g carton cream cheese
200g carton crème fraîche
1 small onion, peeled and finely chopped
2 tablespoons tawny port (use tawny rather than ruby for its colour)
175g Stilton cheese, crumbled
Freshly ground black pepper

A 20cm round, spring clip tin, lined with baking parchment.
Set the oven to fairly hot, Gas Mark 6.

To make the base:
Mix together the breadcrumbs, Parmesan and butter and season well. Press the mixture into the base of the tin only, and bake in the oven for 12-15 minutes or until the crumbs start to turn golden.

Remove and reduce the temperature of the oven to Gas Mark 3.

To make the filling:
Mix together the eggs, cream cheese, crème fraîche, onion and port. Stir in Stilton and season well. Carefully pour this mixture over the base and return to the oven for a further 50-60 min or until the centre of the mix feels firm to touch. Remove from the oven and allow to cool in the tin. Serve warm or cold.

Maureen Johnson ———————————————— Serves 6

Potato and Celeriac Gratin

"No, a mandolin is not just a musical instrument"

450g old potatoes, scrubbed
450g celeriac
1 small onion
285ml single cream
1 clove garlic, crushed
125g sliced smoked ham (Brunswick, if special occasion)
225g Gruyére cheese, grated
Butter for greasing
Salt and pepper

Heat oven to 220°C. Slice potatoes thinly, peel and slice the celeriac and onion. Use food processor or mandolin for ease. Cook celeriac, onion and potatoes together in boiling, lightly salted, water for 3 – 4 minutes.

Meanwhile bring the cream to the boil with the garlic. Drain the vegetables and stir into the hot cream with the ham and all but 60g of cheese. Season. Pour into large shallow, buttered ovenproof dish, such as a lasagne pan. Sprinkle with the rest of the cheese, and cook in oven for 20 minutes or until golden. Serve with French beans.

Caramelised Red Onion Tart

"This can be either a main course or a starter"

1 packet of shortcrust pastry
Butter for frying
1 x 10" loose bottomed flan tin
500g red onions, peeled and thinly sliced
400g of Brie – this does not have to be best quality (Put in the fridge until you are ready to slice it)
75g brown granulated sugar

Fry the onions on a low heat for 10 minutes in a good knob of butter until they have a transparent look, do not let them brown. Add the sugar and continue to cook until the sugar has melted and the onions turn a dark colour – do not brown them.

Roll out the pastry and line the greased flan tin ensuring that the pastry goes right to the top. Prick the base of the pastry with a fork. Bake blind covering the pastry with greaseproof paper and using pastry beans or dried beans for 10 minutes at 180ºC. Remove the beans and cook for a further 5 minutes.

Thinly slice the Brie cheese and line the base of the cooked flan tin. Cover the Brie with the cooked onions and then shake the remaining sugar over the onions.

Cook for 10-15 minutes.

Linda Ruth Williams ———————————————— Serves 4

Euston Frittata

"This is a recipe from an Italian sandwich bar/cafe in Euston. It can be eaten hot or cold, used as a canape, starter or main course."

A 12" diameter x 2½" deep, non-stick frying pan
2 courgettes, chopped roughly
3 lbs of potatoes, peeled and chopped into 1" cubes
2 medium onions, chopped roughly
10 large eggs, beaten and seasoned
3 tablespoons of mature grated cheese
2 tablespoons of fresh chopped oregano
Olive oil for frying

Boil the potatoes until just cooked. Using the olive oil cook the onions in the frying pan until just soft and add the courgettes and cooked potatoes. Fry gently until the courgette has softened. Add the oregano.

Add the beaten eggs, making sure the eggs cover the vegetables.
Cook gently for approximately 8 minutes, or until brown underneath. Just push a pallet knife down the edge and ease the mixture forward to check it.

Remove from the heat and scatter the grated cheese on the top. Place the whole thing under a hot grill until the cheese has browned. The mixture should be firm with no egg liquid visible. Allow to cool slightly, and, being very brave, turn out onto a large plate.

Victoria Fairey

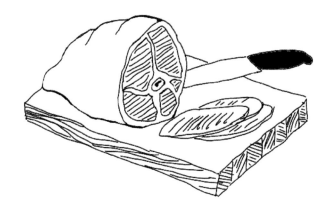

Meat

Mincemeat Stuffed Pork Fillet

"This recipe uses the best that locally sourced ingredients can offer"

4 x 6 oz piece of Bridget B's, or Prior's Hall, fillet of pork
4 oz quality mincemeat
4 pieces Prior's Hall streaky bacon
1 tablespoon oil
3 oz butter
2 chopped shallots
½ teaspoon allspice
4 tablespoons Buntingford Brewery dark mild ale
¼ pint thickened stock
1 tablespoon chopped parsley
Salt and pepper

Cut the pork fillet ½" from one end to ½" from the other, not all the way through to make a pocket in each. Fill with some of the mincemeat. Stretch the streaky bacon using the back of a knife and use this to wrap around the pork to seal the mincemeat in.

Heat the oil in a frying pan and add 1 oz butter. Colour the pork then transfer into a preheated oven at 200°C for 6-8 minutes. Take out and throw away any fat.

Add 1 oz butter to the frying pan and add finely chopped shallots, soften but do not colour. Add allspice, beer and reduce by two thirds. Add stock and bring to the boil. Add the 1 oz butter. Add parsley and check seasoning. To serve, pour sauce over the pork.

Brian Turner – Master Chef - for Food Smiles ———— Serves 4

Food Smiles

Westmill Farm
Westmill Road
Ware
Herts SG12 OES
☎0845 25 76 453
www.foodsmiles.com

Opening Times:
Monday closed
Tuesday, Wednesday, Thursday &
Friday - 10am – 6.00pm
Saturday & Sunday 10am – 4.00pm

A full range of local meat, fresh vegetables, bakery and dairy produce as well as special sauces and condiments. Food Smiles exists to benefit every member of the local food supply chain. We are devoted to making your life easier and offering the highest standards of customer service. Food Smiles is a modern, consumer led business created to fully develop the potential of local food markets.

The Food Smiles shop is within the Three Lakes development at Westmill Farm. It is ideally located 1 mile north of Hertford, and 1 minute by car off the A10 on the A602.

Pork Slosh

1lb pork fillet, cubed
½ oz butter
1 medium onion, finely chopped
4 oz mushrooms, sliced thinly
Salt and white pepper
5 fluid oz double cream
A slosh of dry white wine
½ glass of lemon juice

Melt the butter in pan. Gently fry the onion until opaque. Add mushrooms and fry for 1 minute. Add cubes of pork fillet.

Sauté till slightly brown. Season with salt and pepper. Add double cream. Cook until cream thickens.

Add a good slosh of dry white wine then cook for 20 minutes. Gas Mark 5.

Add the lemon juice just before serving.

Serve with boiled rice or potatoes and green vegetables.

Joyce's Pork Casserole

6 lbs casserole pork or 12 pork steaks
12 onions
Olive oil for frying
Worcestershire sauce
2 green peppers, de-seeded and chopped
Juice of 1 lemon
2 beef stock cubes
2 tins of tomatoes
6 tablespoons tomato purée
1 ½ tablespoons Demerara sugar
3 tablespoons flour
¾ pint water
8 oz mushrooms
Salt and black pepper to taste

Fry pork steaks to brown both sides. Leave to one side.

Fry onions on a low heat to soften. Add 6 shakes of Worcestershire sauce, lemon juice, green pepper, tomatoes and tomato purée and heat.

Stir in flour and gradually add the beef stock. Place pork on top with the mushrooms. Add more water to cover if necessary.

Cook for 3 hours at Gas Mark 3.

Serve with baked or new potatoes and green vegetables.

Liz Horner

Kachee Biryani

200g Basmati rice
Ghee or clarified butter
1 onion, chopped
3 cloves garlic, finely chopped
¼ teaspoon ginger
200g lamb, cut into small pieces
1 tablespoon yogurt
Salt, to season
½ teaspoon turmeric
¼ teaspoon cumin seed powder
¼ teaspoon paprika
1 ½ teaspoon mathi leaves
½ teaspoon curry powder

Marinade the lamb pieces in yogurt and the spices shown above. Heat 2 tablespoons of ghee in a large saucepan and add in ginger and garlic, cook for a few minutes, then add the chopped onion and cook on a medium heat until brown. Stir in the marinated lamb, simmer for 20-30 minutes and cover with lid, stir when necessary and add water if required. When the lamb is tender it is ready.

Prepare the rice whilst lamb is cooking. Wash the rice several times in cold water, drain and then add to the lamb. Stir the rice into the lamb and add in water, enough to cover the surface of the rice by just over half a centimetre. Cover saucepan with lid and simmer for 20 minutes. When the rice and lamb are thoroughly cooked it is ready to be served. Serve alongside with raita, which is yogurt mixed with chopped cucumber, tomatoes, onion and coriander. Season with salt and pepper.

The Neelakash Tandoori Restaurant ——————————— Serves 2

Neelakash Tandoori Restaurant

1-3 Amwell End
Ware
Herts SG12 9HV
☎01920 487038 & 487807

Opening times:
7 days a week
12.00 - 2.30pm &
6.00pm – Midnight

Located near the river crossing, a friendly restaurant loved by many. Indian restaurant serving authentic dishes. Fresh ingredients with food to suit all palates. An extensive wine list. Fully licensed and air conditioned. Master Chef Award and European Food and Drink Award Winner. Buffet and Take Away service available.

Shepherd's Pie

900g potatoes, peeled and quartered
350g lean, minced lamb
1 large onion, chopped finely
1 large leek, chopped finely
1 carrot chopped
225g swede or turnip, chopped
450ml lamb or vegetable stock
2 tablespoons cornflour, blended with 3 or 4 tablespoons cold water
6 tablespoons skimmed milk
Salt and freshly ground black pepper

Cook the potatoes in lightly salted boiling water for about 20 minutes until tender. Meanwhile, heat a large non-stick saucepan and add the lamb mince, a handful at a time, cooking over a high heat to seal and brown it. Add the onion to the mince with the leek, carrot and swede or turnip and cook for about 3 minutes, stirring often. Pour in the stock, bring to the boil. Cover and simmer for about 20 minutes.

Preheat the oven to Gas Mark 5. Stir the blended cornflour into the minced lamb mixture. Cook until thickened for about 2 minutes. Remove from the heat.

Drain the potatoes and mash them. Add the milk and seasoning and beat vigorously with a wooden spoon until the potatoes are light and fluffy. Alternatively, use a hand-held electric beater to whisk the potatoes for a few moments. Transfer the meat mixture to a 1.2 ltr ovenproof dish and top with the mashed potato. Bake for 25-30 minutes until thoroughly heated and browned.

Poussins Marsala

3 poussins or 6 chicken breasts
2 oz butter
¼ pint marsala or sherry
¼ pint double cream
2-3 cloves garlic, crushed
4 oz cheddar cheese, grated
chopped parsley
¼ teaspoon paprika

Fry the poussins in butter for 5 minutes until golden. Drain off the fat.

Return to heat, pour over marsala. Top with a tightly fitting lid and bubble gently for about 40 minutes.

Whip the cream, fold in garlic and cheese, paprika and salt and pepper.

Transfer poussins to a gratin dish. Spoon creamy mixture over and flash under a hot grill.

Serve sprinkled with parsley.

Anne Lloyd-Skinner

Serves 6   53

Spinach & Pork Terrine à la Liz

"This can be served either as a main course or part of a buffet"

1lb fresh spinach or 9 oz frozen
8 rashers of streaky bacon
12 oz lean belly pork, diced
1lb sausage meat
1 medium chopped onion
2 garlic cloves, peeled and crushed
2 eggs
Salt and pepper
½ teaspoon ground nutmeg
6-7 oz sliced cooked ham, cut into finger sized pieces
2 teaspoons of whole green peppercorns

Cook the spinach until just tender and drain. Line a 2¾ pint terrine dish with bacon. Mince the belly pork.

Add the sausage meat and work in the onion, garlic, eggs, salt, pepper and nutmeg and mix well.

Add the spinach but don't over mix, spoon half the mixture into the terrine, cover with pieces of ham and peppercorns, then spoon in rest of mixture and smooth the top.

Place the terrine in a roasting tin with water a third of the way up the side. Place in oven Gas Mark 5 for 1¼ to 1½ hours.

To serve cold, cover the terrine with greaseproof paper and then a heavy weight. Chill.

Serves 6 to 12

Tarragon Chicken with Herby Potatoes

4 chicken breasts, boned
100ml double cream
Handful tarragon sprigs
25g butter
1 tablespoon groundnut oil
500ml chicken stock

Melt the butter in a heavy-based skillet or saucepan, adding the oil when the butter begins to sizzle. Add the chicken breasts and cook over a medium heat for 3-4 minutes. (Until starting to brown.) Turn the chicken and cook for a further 3 minutes. Add the chicken stock and tarragon (reserving some for garnish). Continue to cook for 10 minutes.

The chicken should be cooked through and the stock reduced by half. Remove the chicken and keep warm. Remove the tarragon and dispose of it. Add the cream and reduce the heat to low for 1-2 minutes. Serve the chicken dressed with sauce and tarragon sprigs, herby potatoes and green vegetables.

Herby potatoes – Dice enough potato (Maris Piper) for 4 and put in a roasting tin. Sprinkle with olive oil, sea salt and chopped herbs of your choice. (Rosemary, thyme and lavender work well.) Cook in a pre-heated oven at 200°C for 20 – 30 minutes - turning occasionally.

Hilary Clark ———————————————————— Serves 4   55

Melitzanes Papoutsakia

"Melitzanes Papoutsakia translates to Aubergine Little Shoes"

2 aubergines
2 soupspoons olive oil
1 medium onion
500g minced meat (lamb, pork or beef)
2 tomatoes, skinned and chopped
1 soupspoon tomato paste
½ teaspoon thyme
½ teaspoon mint (fresh or dried)
½ teaspoon ground cinnamon
Salt and pepper
For the cheese sauce:
30g butter
25g flour
½ pint full fat milk
Dash ground cinnamon
1 teaspoon orange liqueur (optional)

Cut the aubergine in half and with a soupspoon take out the flesh. Cook the minced meat in a saucepan with the oil and onions, tomatoes and herbs.

Deep fry the aubergine skins and place them on kitchen paper to absorb excess oil. Melt the butter in a saucepan and stir in the flour, then gradually stir in the milk. Stir until thick and smooth.

Fill each aubergine with mince meat and place sauce over top, sprinkle with cheese. You may add the liqueur to the sauce when it is ready. Bake them in the oven at 180°C until brown.

The Village Taverna

42-44 West Street
Ware
Herts SG12 9EE
☎01920 468931
www.villagetaverna.co.uk

Opening Times:
Lunch: Tuesday - Saturday 12.00 - 3.00pm
Evenings: Monday – Saturday 6.00 – 11.00pm

A Greek Restaurant overlooking a pretty town garden.
Fully licensed and air-conditioned.
The menu is simple, authentic and ingredient driven.
The food is fresh, the atmosphere is friendly, and the staff welcoming. Exactly how good Greek restaurants should be.

Braised Lamb Shanks with Flageolet Beans

1 tablespoon vegetable oil
4 lamb braising shanks
1 onion, chopped
1 large carrot, chopped
1 stick celery, chopped
1 x 400g can chopped tomatoes
½ pint lamb stock
2 bay leaves
3 sprigs rosemary
2 x 300g cans flageolet beans, drained

Preheat the oven to 160°C. Heat the oil in a flameproof casserole and brown the lamb shanks on all sides. Remove them from the dish.

Add the onion, carrot, and celery to the pan, and cook until the onion is translucent. Tip in the tomatoes, stock and herbs, then bring to a simmer.

Add the lamb shanks, and season generously. Cover and cook in the centre of the oven for 1½ hours.

Stir in the beans and return to the oven for a further 30 minutes. Serve with spring vegetables.

Pat Collin ———————————————————————— Serves 4

Leek and Ham Gallette

700g medium leeks, cut into
¾" slices
50g butter
50g plain flour
100ml milk
2 tablespoons chopped fresh
marjoram
100g Beaufort or Gruyère
cheese, cubed
4 level tablespoons grated
cheese
2 x 150g packs good quality
cooked, sliced ham thickly
shredded
Plain flour to dust
1 x 425g pack chilled puff
pastry, two sheets
1 egg beaten with pinch of
salt
¾ pint leek water

Preheat oven to 220°C. Cook the leeks in water for 2-3 minutes until softened. D... reserving the li... Plunge leeks into cold water and drain thoroughly until...

Melt butter in large pan. Mix in the flour. Add the leek water, and milk, stirring until smooth. Bring to boil, then simmer for 1-2 minutes. Cool until cold. Add marjoram, leeks, cubed cheese, and ham. Season to taste.

On a floured surface, roll out one sheet of pastry. Cut into two rectangles, 6"x 12" And 7" x 12 Repeat with the other sheet. Put the two smaller rectangles onto two greased baking sheets. Spoon on the ham mixture, leaving a ¼" border. Brush the edges with beaten egg. Cover the filling with the remaining rectangles and press edges together firmly. Crimp the edges. Cut several slashes in the top of the pastry. Cover and freeze for 20 minutes until firm.

Remove, brush with beaten egg. Cut a good sized steam hole in the centre of each, and sprinkle with grated cheese. Bake for 20-30 minutes.

Venison in Red Wine

"This is good served with braised red cabbage and herb dumplings"

700g casserole venison, cut into decent sized cubes
2 carrots, chopped into chunks
¼ swede, chopped into chunks
6-8 shallots, peeled and left whole
2 tomatoes, cut into quarters
150ml red wine
450ml stock
¼ teaspoon mixed herbs
Seasoned flour
Salt and pepper

Shake the meat and vegetables in seasoned flour, and then fry in a little oil for a few minutes until browned. Transfer to a casserole dish.

Add stock, wine, herbs and season well with salt and pepper. Place in the oven and cook on 200°C until bubbling, then turn down to 150°C until meat is tender (about 2 hours).

R. Gannon Family Butcher ———— Serves 4

R. Gannon Family Butcher

2A East Street
Ware
Herts SG12 9HJ
☎01920 485641

Opening times:
Monday 7.30am – 1pm
Tuesday, Wednesday,
Thursday, Friday 7.30am – 5pm
Saturday 7.30am – 2pm

Home made sausages, cooked meats and
hams. The source of all meat is identified and
local produce is always available. Fresh
Beef, Pork, Lamb, Poultry & Game.
We offer good old fashioned service.

Chicken and Almonds

"Given to me by a friend when we lived in Brunei. Easy to prepare for entertaining or a family meal."

1 chicken, jointed or in pieces
2-3 oz butter
1 dessertspoon olive oil
2 onions
3 tomatoes, skinned, deseeded and shredded
15 fl oz chicken stock
3 oz blanched almonds
2 oz sultanas
Cinnamon
Seasoning

Heat butter and oil in pan and brown chicken quickly on all sides.

Peel and chop onions and add to the pan with the tomatoes.
Season and add a good pinch of cinnamon.
Cook gently for 10 minutes turning the chicken frequently. Pour in the stock and cover with a pan lid.

Simmer gently for 20 minutes or pour into a hot casserole dish, cover and cook in the oven at 180°C for 20 minutes.

Check the seasoning and then pile the chicken onto a hot dish and pour the sauce over it. Serve with boiled rice.

Kath Kirby ———————————————— Serves 4

Chicken Fajitas

"Guacamole, salsa or soured cream dips go well with this dish."

1 skinless chicken breast
Rind of 2 limes and 1 lemon
2 tablespoons caster sugar
½ onion, cut into 1 cm cubes
3 bell peppers (red, orange and green), deseeded and cut into 1 cm cubes
Juice of l lemon and 1 lime.

Tortillas:
200g plain flour
pinch of salt
25g margarine
20ml warm water

Slice the chicken into 2 cm strips then place into a bowl. Add the lemon and lime rind and juice. Leave to marinade for least 30 minutes (longer the better).

To make the tortillas mix the flour and salt in a mixing bowl. Rub in the margarine. Add the warm water a little at a time until a stiff dough is achieved. Knead for about 10 minutes until the dough is elastic. Divide the dough in half and roll out into 2 x 15 cm circles. Then cover with clingflim. Heat a large frying pan with a little of the oil and when the pan is hot add the tortilla. Cook for about 1 minute on each side. After cooking cover with clingfilm or keep warm otherwise the tortillas will go hard.

Heat a frying pan with some of the oil and add the onion and peppers. Sweat gently then add the marinaded chicken. Cook for about 5 minutes then add half the marinade and turn down the heat and cook for a further 5 - 6 minutes.
Spoon out the filling from the pan and serve with the warmed tortillas.

Dane Barnard – a student at Chauncy School ——————— Serves 2   63

Ghalina Cafreal

"What better way to capture a glimpse of an Indian summer than to sit in the garden and enjoy a barbeque. This dish was inherited by the Portuguese in Mozambique and then transported to Goa. Our cafreal is the Goan version with a few variations"

450g chicken breasts, cut into 2.5cm cubes
25g fresh mint
25g fresh coriander
1 green chilli
100g natural yogurt
1 tablespoon of garlic pulp
1 teaspoon of ginger pulp
1 egg yolk
1 teaspoon of garam masala
1 teaspoon of salt (or to your taste)
1 tablespoon of freshly squeezed lemon juice
1 teaspoon of mustard oil
1 teaspoon of coriander powder (optional)
1 teaspoon of cumin powder (optional)

Rinse the chicken under cold water and leave in colander to drain for 10 minutes. Blend the mint, coriander and green chilli to a fine green paste and set aside. Mix the yogurt with the garlic and ginger pulp, egg yolk, garam masala, cumin and coriander powder. Add this to the green paste prepared earlier. Mix all the ingredients well together. Add salt and the chicken pieces, cover and put into the refrigerator for about 12 hours to marinate.

Bring marinated chicken out of the fridge 10 minutes before cooking. The chicken can either be skewered and cooked over charcoal or arranged on a greased baking tray and cooked under a grill, or inside an oven. The tikkas will take about 10 – 12 minutes to cook.

Le Spice Merchant

Flutes House
14 High Street
Ware
Herts SG12 9BX
☎01920 468383
www.lespicemerchant.co.uk

Opening Times:
7 days a week
(including bank holidays)
Lunch 12pm – 3 pm
Dinner 6 pm - 12 pm

Always well reviewed by Ware
residents, Le Spice Merchant
has its own signature dishes but also serves popular and traditional dishes to suit all palates and
taste buds. Take Away and delivery service available.

Pan Fried Calves' Liver

4 x 125g calves' livers
25g butter
4 tablespoons crème fraîche
Juice of ½ lemon

Cut the livers into 1 cm or ½" strips – never thicker, never thinner. Heat a heavy-based frying pan until hot. Add half the butter and allow to sizzle.

Season the liver on both sides, then add to the pan. Cook for 1 minute on each side, adding the remaining butter as you turn the liver.

Take the liver out of the pan and keep warm. Turn the heat down, then add the crème fraîche and lemon juice to the pan. Swirl the pan around so the crème fraîche melts, then pour the sauce over the liver.

Serve with potato and steamed greens.

Pat Collin ———————————————————————— Serves 4

Beef Casserole

675g Braising steak, cut into 1½" cubes
30ml sunflower oil
8 small shallots, peeled and left whole
1 large garlic clove, chopped
1 large carrot, peeled and thickly sliced
30g plain flour
600ml good beef stock
300ml good red wine
15ml red wine vinegar
2 large sprigs thyme
2 bay leaves
15ml golden syrup

Heat the oil in a large non-stick frying pan and cook the meat for 4 - 5 minutes in batches, and spoon into a large casserole dish.

Add the shallots, garlic and carrots to the pan and cook for 2 - 3 minutes. Stir in the flour and cook for a further 1 - 2 minutes. Transfer to the casserole dish.

Add the stock, wine, vinegar and herbs to the casserole dish and stir in the golden syrup.

Cover and cook in the oven for 1 - 1½ hrs stirring occasionally. Gas Mark 3.

Joan Peel ——————————————— Serves 4   67

Beef and Stilton Grills

"This is a very rich meat dish and uses a particular cut of beef called a 'Leg of Mutton' cut which is from the rear leg of the animal"

2 x 4 oz slices of beef leg of mutton cut
4 oz of lean mince
1 dessertspoon of olive oil
A pinch of ground cloves and cumin
2 pieces of stilton cheese, 2 oz each
Salt and freshly ground pepper

Flatten out each slice of beef placing the beef between two pieces of baking parchment.

Mix the mince with the oil and spices. Place a piece of stilton inside the mince mixture in one piece and fold the flattened beef around the filling. Repeat for the second piece of beef.

This recipe is suitable for the oven grill, barbecue or frying. Cook for 8 minutes on each side. Alternatively, roast in a preheated oven at 180°C wrapped in tin foil and cook for 20 minutes.

G.S. Pickett Family Butchers ———————————————— Serves 2

G. S. Pickett Family Butchers

The Green
Kingshill
Ware
Herts SG12 0QW
☎01920 463240

Opening Times:
6.00am – 5.00pm Monday to
Friday
6.00am – 4.00pm Saturday

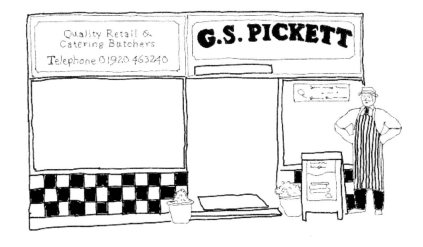

A very popular, traditional
butcher who has been serving
Ware people for many years.
Barbecue and marinated meats a specialty. Cold meats, cheese, eggs and sauces are also
available. Meat prepared for parties and fund-raising events.

Sausages with Puy Lentils

16-20 good quality sausages – any flavour
275g puy lentils
Streaky smoked bacon
4 shallots finely chopped
6-8 sprigs of thyme,
1 tablespoon redcurrant jelly
2 tins beef consommé
sherry (about a glass full)
4 tablespoons crème fraîche

Fry bacon and shallots in large ovenproof casserole. Grill sausages separately. Add Puy lentils to frying pan, add sausages.

Add thyme and consommé and sherry. Cook unlidded for 35 minutes on hob, or covered for 45 minutes in oven at 200°C.

Stir in crème fraîche and redcurrant jelly. Serve with mashed potatoes and green vegetables.

Anne Lloyd-Skinner ————————————————— Serves 6

Alan's Chorizo and Smoky Bacon Risotto

100g good quality chorizo
100g smoky bacon bits
1 cup long grain rice
1 onion
1 red pepper, de-seeded and chopped
3 cloves garlic (optional)
1 green chilli, de-seeded and chopped
1 tin tomatoes
2 cups water
2 tablespoons tomato purée
1 tablespoon balsamic vinegar
Paprika
Cayenne pepper
Oregano (fresh if possible)
Juice from 1 lemon
Black pepper
Green peppercorns
Olive oil to fry

Fry bacon, onion, crushed garlic and chorizo in oil until softened.

Stew down, after adding tomatoes and tomato purée. Add pepper, chilli, spices and oregano (if dried add now, if fresh leave until near to end of cooking). Add rice and water, and then add lemon juice and vinegar.

Cook for 15 minutes on a moderate heat. Serve alone or with green salad.

Liz Horner

Cheesy Topped Cottage Pie

"This is very versatile and can be used as a base for lasagne, a pie filling or served with herby dumplings. Make in small dishes for children. This is one of our popular dishes. Enjoy"

1 tablespoon oil
1¼ lb beef mince (we buy ours from Pickett's)
14 oz can chopped tomatoes
4 Oxo cubes, crumbled
½ pint of hot water
A large cooking onion, finely chopped
2 medium carrots, chopped
2 bay leaves
About 4 springs of fresh thyme
3 tablespoons tomato purée
Salt and freshly ground black pepper

For the cheesey mash topping:
2 lb potatoes, peeled and chopped
2½ oz butter
1 fl oz milk
4 oz strong Cheddar cheese, grated

Preheat the oven to 190°C. Heat the oil in a big frying pan. (A wok is good.) Fry the onion and carrot until soft. Not too high or the onions may burn. This should take about 5 or 6 minutes.
Then add minced beef, and cook until nice and brown. This may take about 5 minutes. Mix in the crumbled Oxo cubes, tinned tomatoes and purée, bay leaves, and seasoning herbs. Then add about ½ pint water. Cover and simmer for 30 minutes, or you can put this mixture in your slow cooker. Adjust seasoning to taste.

To make the mash: boil the potatoes until soft. Drain and mash with the butter and milk. Mix in half the cheese and season with salt and pepper. Spoon the meat into an ovenproof dish. Put the mash on the top and sprinkle with the remaining cheese. Bake in the oven until nice and crispy.

"This freezes well."

The Tap Bar

High Street
Ware
Herts SG12 9AD
☎01920 485315
www.thetapbar.co.uk

Food opening times:
Monday to Friday 8.30am – 10.00pm
Saturday 9.00am – 10.00pm
Sunday 9.30 – 10.00pm

The Tap Bar is a family run business. We offer a
warm welcome to everyone. We serve food all day
from breakfast to lunch, to afternoon tea and
dinner, with ice cream sundaes whenever you like.
You are also welcome to just have tea or coffee or
a beer if you want. We also have four very nice bed
and breakfast rooms.

Peasant Pork

1¼ lb pork fillet
1 oz butter
1 tablespoon corn oil
3 medium onions, sliced
2 cloves garlic, crushed (optional)
12 oz tomatoes, skinned and quartered
8 oz mushrooms
Salt and pepper
1 tablespoon tomato purée
1 teaspoon dried basil
¼ pint soured cream
Chopped parsley to garnish

Trim the pork fillet and cut into 1 inch cubes.

Melt the butter and oil in a large saucepan and fry the pork quickly to lightly brown and seal in the juices. Add the onions, garlic, tomatoes, mushrooms, seasoning, tomato purée and basil. Blend thoroughly.

Cover and cook slowly for 30 minutes or until the meat is tender.

Stir in the soured cream, garnish with parsley and serve with cooked rice or noodles.

Pat Collin ————— Serves 4

Chicken Dagmar

1 chicken or 8 thighs, skinned
4 oz butter
2 tablespoons flour
10 fl oz thick cream
¾ pint chicken stock
1 teaspoon curry powder
3 oz mushrooms
8 oz breadcrumbs
4 oz cheese
1 lemon
12 peppercorns
1 chopped onion (optional)
1 tablespoon parsley, chopped
flaked almonds to decorate (optional)

Rub chicken with lemon and boil with parsley, onion, 12 peppercorns, and salt. Boil until cooked then leave to cool.

When cold, debone and cut meat into bite-sized pieces. Put in a baking dish approximately 8" x 12".

Slice mushrooms and cook in some of the butter. Spread over chicken and make a sauce with 2 oz of the butter, flour, curry powder and stock. Add cream then pour over chicken.

Spread over the breadcrumbs which have been mixed with grated cheese.
Use remaining butter and put knobs over the top.
Bake in a moderate oven for about 45 minutes.

Kaeng Matsaman Neua

"This curry has many characteristics of southern Thai cooking. Sweet flavours and spices dominate, even though the curry is moderately hot. It also has a sour taste from the tamarind. This dish is one of the few Thai dishes with potatoes and peanuts"

2 pieces of cinnamon sticks
10 cardamom seeds
5 cloves
2 tablespoons vegetable oil
2 tablespoons massaman curry paste
800g beef flank or top side, cut into 5cm cubes
410ml coconut milk
250ml beef stock
2 – 3 potatoes, cut into 2.5 cm pieces
3 tablespoons fish sauce
3 tablespoons palm sugar
110g roasted salted peanuts
3 tablespoons tamarind purée

Dry fry the cinnamon stick, cardamom seeds and cloves in a saucepan or wok over low heat. Stir all the ingredients around for 2 to 3 minutes or until fragrant. Remove from pan.

Heat the oil in the same saucepan or wok and stir fry the massaman paste over medium heat for 2 minutes or until fragrant.

Add the beef to the pan and stir for 5 minutes. Add the coconut milk, stock, potatoes, fish sauce, palm sugar, three quarters of the peanuts, tamarind puree, and the dry-fried spices. Reduce the heat to low, and gently simmer for 50 to 60 minutes until the meat is tender, and the potatoes are just cooked. Taste, then adjust the seasoning if necessary. Spoon into a serving bowl and garnish with the rest of the roasted peanuts. Serve with steamed Jasmine rice.

Serves 4

Sala Thai Restaurant

34 High Street
Ware
Herts SG12 9BY
☎01920 463519
www.salathaiware.co.uk

Open 7 days a week
Tuesday – Saturday 12.00 – 2.30pm
& 6.00 - 11.00pm
Sunday & Monday   12.00 – 2.30pm
& 6.00 - 10.30pm

Royal Thai Cuisine. Wonderful Thai food
served in a romantic setting. Our chefs
use only the freshest authentic ingredients
in every dish.

We are a family run business and have a
common goal, that is to bring the cooking
of our country and its associated levels of
attention and service to the diners of
Ware.

Puddings

Rhubarb & Apple Pudding

"For special occasions instead of bread this traditional recipe could be made with brioche"

4-8 slices good quality bread
Butter
8 oz rhubarb or apples
2 oz sultanas
Pinch of nutmeg
3 oz brown or demerara sugar
¼ teaspoon ground ginger
2 eggs
¾ pint milk

Place bread (buttered if desired), fruit, sugar and sultanas in a greased dish in alternate layers. Finish with buttered bread on top.

Beat eggs, add milk, nutmeg and ginger and pour over.

Cook in moderate 180°C oven for approximately ¾ hour.

Zara Kimber ─────────────── Serves 4

Katy's Key Lime Pie

"This is so easy"

375g ginger nut biscuits
150g unsalted butter
8 limes – zest and juice
1 pint double cream
397g tin of condensed milk

Crush the biscuits to a fine powder. Melt the butter over a low heat, and combine with the biscuit mixture.

Spread evenly into a loose bottom 8" flan tin and leave to cool.

Meanwhile, combine the cream, milk and juice of the limes and whisk for 2 minutes. Add the zest.

Pour over the cooled base and spread evenly. Leave to cool and set.

For garnish grate some dark chocolate over the pie.

Sugar-grilled Clementines with Gin ————

"You can use gin or vodka for the recipe. You may substitute the alcohol with the juice of two extra clementines"

6 – 8 clementines with leaves
1 oz unsalted butter
4 tablespoons soft brown sugar
3 tablespoons gin or vodka

Peel the skin and pith from the clementines. Thinly shred the peel of one clementine. Set aside the leaves.

In a large pan melt the butter with 3 tablespoons of the sugar. Add the whole clementines and the shredded peel, then cover the pan with a lid and cook for 2 minutes. Add the gin or vodka, cover the pan again and cook for 1 more minute.

Place the clementines in an ovenproof dish, pour over the juice and shredded peel. Sprinkle over the remaining sugar. Place under a grill on a low heat and cook until the sugar starts to caramelise. Leave to cook for a few minutes.

Eat on their own or with vanilla ice cream. Serve decorated with the clementine leaves.

Pat Collin ————— Serves 2

1 large lemon
5 fl oz medium white wine
3 oz caster sugar
10 fl oz double cream
2 egg whites
1 orange and 1 lime for
decoration

Finely grate the lemon rind. Place in a small bowl with 3 tablespoons of lemon juice, the wine and sugar. Leave to stand for about 15 minutes or until the sugar has dissolved. Stir occasionally.

Whip the cream until it holds its shape. Add about 4 tablespoons of the wine mixture at a time, whisking well after each addition to ensure the cream thickens slightly again, and will just hold its shape. Whisk the egg whites until they stand in soft peaks. Gently fold the egg whites into the wine mixture. Carefully spoon the syllabub into six tall glasses. Cover and refrigerate for at least 2 hours or overnight before serving.

Meanwhile, using a potato peeler, pare a little rind off the orange and lime. Scrape off any white pith, then cut the rind into very fine shreds. Blanch in boiling water for 1 min. Drain in a nylon sieve and run under the cold tap. Dry on kitchen paper and sprinkle a little over each syllabub on serving.

Crème Brûlée

"This is always popular on our menu and is easy to adapt by adding seasonal fruit"

300ml double cream
200ml full fat milk
7 egg yolks
3½ tablespoons of caster sugar
1 vanilla pod
Extra caster sugar for the topping

Whisk the cream, sugar, milk and egg yolks until you have a smooth mixture with the consistency of single cream.

Split the vanilla pod and scrape out the black seeds and add to the mixture.

Divide the mixture evenly between heat proof ramekins and cook in a bain marie in an oven for about 1½ hours at 180°C until just set. Leave to cool.

Just before serving, when the crème is cooled sprinkle an even layer of caster sugar on the surface of each ramekin and caramelise. For best results use a chef's blow torch. If not available, use a hot grill.

The Vine Restaurant & Wine Bar

22 High Street
Ware
Herts SG12 9BY
☎01920 462462
vineware@gmail.com

Food is served:
Monday – Saturday 12.00-3pm
& 6.00 – 9.30pm
Sunday 12.00 – 7.30pm
Open for drinks 11am – 11pm

The dining rooms can be enjoyed
at any time of day or night.

The Vine has a traditional yet
contemporary feel. The menu
specialises in traditional British dishes with an international flavour, and home made hearty
puddings, that keep everyone happy.

Chocolate Coffee Cups

"This is a very easy chocolate pudding to make and derives from a Nigella Lawson recipe who said she got it from someone else who got it from someone else. You could use any good dark chocolate but I think the Maya Gold just adds that extra taste of orange and spice"

175g of Green & Black's Maya Gold Chocolate
150ml of double cream
100ml of semi-skimmed milk
½ teaspoon of vanilla extract
¼ teaspoon of allspice
1 egg
8 small coffee cups

Using a food processor, chop the chocolate until it is in tiny pieces.

Heat the cream and the milk until just under boiling. Add the vanilla and the allspice and pour through the funnel of the processor. Let the mixture stand for 30 seconds. Process for 30 seconds. Add the egg. Process for 45 seconds.

Pour into the coffee cups. This does seem like a small portion but honestly it is very rich. Let the cups rest for half a day in a fridge or overnight. Remove from the fridge 20 minutes before serving. Serve as they are or with an amaretto biscuits and cream.

for Olive Woodhouse ——————————— Serves 8

Apple & Lemon Tart

"This recipe is easy using a food processor but it can be made just as easily by hand. It is an Italian recipe"

1 large apple, peeled and cored
Grated rind and juice of 1 lemon
3 eggs
75g butter
75g caster sugar
Whipped cream to serve
225g of dessert pastry
10" flan tin

Roll out the pastry and line a greased, loose bottomed, flan tin. Prick the pastry with a fork. Bake blind using paper and beans at 200°C for 6-10 minutes.

Remove paper and beans, and bake for a further 5 minutes. Place the apple in the food processor and chop for a few seconds until roughly chopped. Remove and add to the lemon juice and grated rind.

Put the sugar, butter and eggs into the processor, (no need to clean after the apples) and beat well. Add the apples and lemon juice to the mixture and process for another 20 seconds. Pour the mixture into the cooked pastry case and cook for 20 minutes at 160°C; it should be golden on top but not brown.

Allow to cool slightly before removing from the tin. Serve with whipped cream.

Victoria Fairey — Serves 8   87

Pineapple and Ginger Tart

"This is a good recipe if you need a pudding in a hurry"

For the base:

6 oz ginger biscuits
3 oz butter
A flan tin (8" or 9") preferably with a
loose base or line the tin with cooking
foil.

For the filling:

3 level tablespoons ginger preserve (or
orange marmalade)
1 tin crushed pineapple
¼ pint double cream

Crush the biscuits either in a food processor or place in a polythene bag and crush with a rolling pin. Melt the butter in a pan and stir in the biscuit crumbs.

Put the mixture into a tin and press it firmly to the base with a potato masher. When the base is cold (this process can be speeded up by placing the tin in the fridge) spread it with the ginger preserve.

Whip the cream until it will hold its shape then mix in the crushed pineapple – keep some aside for decoration. Smooth over the surface. Leave for a short time in the fridge, then slip the sides off the tin. Decorate the top with a ring of crushed pineapple.

Kath Kirby ———————————————— Serves 6

2 eggs
2 oz caster sugar
2 oz self-raising flour
1 tablespoon boiling water
550ml of double cream
Fresh or frozen fruit

Preheat oven to Gas Mark 6. Line a Swiss roll tin with baking paper. Sprinkle a second piece with caster sugar.

Beat the eggs for 30 seconds on fast speed. Add sugar and beat on fast speed for 3 minutes until thick and creamy and beaters leave a trail. Gently fold in flour. Add boiling water and pour mixture into prepared tin until it completely covers the bottom of tin. Bake in the top of the oven for 10 minutes.

When cooked, turn out immediately onto prepared second paper and gently peel off the first lining paper. Cut off the sides of the sponge and roll up with the sugar covered paper and leave to get cold. Very gently unroll.

Beat double cream until thick but not solid. If the fruit is sharp add one teaspoon of icing sugar to the cream. Spread the cream mixture over the sponge. Gently place drained or fresh fruit on top of the cream but leave a margin which will be the outer edge of the Swiss roll. Re-roll, sprinkle with extra caster sugar and put in fridge until serving.

Creamy Chocolate Mousse Pie

"This recipe is quick to make"

18 Chocolate Digestive biscuits
25g butter or margarine, melted
600ml skimmed milk
2 pack (4 servings each) sugar free instant
chocolate dessert mix
1 teaspoon vanilla extract
½ teaspoon instant espresso powder
250ml light whipped topping

Pre-heat oven to 190ºC.
Crush the digestive biscuits into crumbs.
Combine the crumbs and butter and press
onto a 9" pie plate. Press firmly and bake for
6 minutes. Cool completely on a rack.

In a large bowl whisk together the milk,
dessert mix, vanilla extract and espresso
powder for 2 minutes or until smooth and
creamy. Whip the topping and fold into the
mixture.

Spoon over the prepared crumb crust. Cover
and refrigerate for at least 3 hours.

Joan Rees ⸺⸺⸺⸺⸺⸺⸺ Serves 10

Rhubarb & Ginger Cheesecake

"This is a wonderful dish for the summer, it should have a slight pink colour – do not be tempted to use 'light' cream cheese because it will not set"

7 oz ginger biscuits, broken
2 oz butter, melted
14 oz full fat cheese
2 oz icing sugar
3 oz stem ginger, chopped
1 lb fresh, pink rhubarb (or 560g tin in syrup), drained

Melt butter and add broken biscuits and crush. Press into base of loose-bottomed 7" cake tin. Refrigerate for 15 minutes.

Mix together the cream cheese, icing sugar, stem ginger and rhubarb.

Spread mixture over base and put in fridge for at least 2 hours.

Garnish with fresh fruit, perhaps sliced strawberries and mint leaves.

Jo Ransome

Cakes & Things

Barm Brack

12 fl oz cold tea
7 oz soft brown sugar
12 oz mixed dried fruit
10 oz self raising flour
1 egg

Pre-heat oven to Gas Mark 4.

Put tea, sugar and dried fruit in a bowl, cover and soak overnight. Tea that has been left over during the soaking should be saved. Well grease an 8" round cake tin or a 2 lb loaf tin.

Mix the soaked fruit and sugar plus the saved tea into a bowl. Add the flour and beaten egg to make a smooth mixture. Turn out into a tin and bake in a moderate oven for about l hour 45 minutes. Turn out and cool on a wire tray.

Serve sliced with butter.

Coconut Chocolate

10 oz of good quality cooking chocolate
1 cupful of desiccated coconut
1 cupful caster sugar
1 medium egg
12 Glacé cherries

Melt chocolate and pour into a shallow tin (a Swiss roll tin is ideal), and allow to set.

Cream egg and sugar together and beat well. Add coconut and mix well. Press the coconut mixture on to set chocolate. Push around to make it cover all the chocolate.

Cut cherries in half and put on top of coconut mix. Depending on how big you want the squares to be put the cherries on each intended square. Put into a pre-heated oven Gas Mark 4 and cook until golden brown – approximately 20 minutes. Leave to cool.

Cut into squares when cold. This keeps well in an airtight tin.

Mary Briant

Makes 24 squares

Balmoral Cake

4 oz butter or soft margarine
4 oz caster sugar
½ teaspoon almond essence
2 eggs, beaten
2 oz ground almonds
7 oz plain flour
2 teaspoons baking powder
1 tablespoon milk

For the icing:
4 oz icing sugar
2 oz butter or soft margarine
Almond essence (a tiny drop)
Toasted almond flakes

Set oven at 170°C. Beat butter with sugar until light and fluffy. Add beaten eggs and almond essence. Fold in flour, baking powder, ground almonds, then milk.

Bake in the middle of the oven for 20 minutes at 170°C, then 25 minutes at 140°C. Leave to cool then turn cake out leaving it upside down.

Combine all the icing ingredients together and pour over upside cake. Decorate with almond flakes.

Carrot Cake

"This cake freezes very well so slice it up and bag individually"

275g soft brown sugar
1 large can prunes, stoned and puréed
Grated rind of 1 orange
4 eggs
400g self-raising flour
2 teaspoons baking powder
1 teaspoon each of ginger, mixed spice and ground nutmeg
450g carrots, peeled and finely grated (almost puréed)
175g sultanas

Preheat the oven to Gas Mark 4. Lightly grease and line a 10" round cake tin.

Using a large bowl, cream together the sugar, prunes and orange rind. Gradually beat in the eggs. Reserve the juice from the tin of prunes for later.

Fold in the flour and the remaining ingredients, a little at a time.
Finally, fold in the grated carrots and sultanas. If the mixture seems a little too stiff, slacken it with the juice that the prunes were in. Transfer into the prepared tin and bake in the oven for 1 to 1¼ hours. Leave to cool in the tin.

Sheila Steele

Almond Cake

"This recipe makes a 7½" - 8" round cake. This is a moist cake that will keep for up to 2 weeks if wrapped in foil and stored in an air tight container in a cool place"

8 oz butter or softened margarine
8 oz caster sugar
4 medium eggs, beaten
2 tablespoons milk
7 oz self-raising flour
8 oz ground almonds

Grease the tin and pre-heat the oven to Gas Mark 3.

Cream butter and sugar until light and fluffy. Gradually add the eggs, beating well and after each addition beat in some milk and 1 tablespoon of the flour. Fold in the remaining flour and ground almonds. Spoon into the tin, level the surface then make a slight hollow in the centre.

Bake in the centre of the oven for 1 hour 35 minutes or until golden and firm. Allow to stand for 10 minutes in the tin. Carefully transfer to a wire rack.

Orange Tea Bread

"A recipe given for a competition in Much Hadam for the annual Horticultural Show – I didn't win but it tastes nice."

6 oz self-raising flour
3 oz caster sugar
1 orange
2 tablespoons milk
1 tablespoon chunky marmalade
1 egg
Pinch of salt
1 tablespoon cooking oil

Sieve together the flour and salt.
Add sugar, sultanas, grated rind of orange, marmalade, oil, egg and milk. Mix well.

Turn into a well greased small loaf tin. Bake for 45 – 50 minutes at 180°C

Serve with butter.

Kath Kirby

Moist Fruit Loaf

"A traditional recipe evoking memories of high tea"

6 oz self-raising flour
6 oz mixed fruit, sultanas or raisins
1 oz caster sugar
2 tablespoons black treacle
5 fl oz good quality natural yogurt

Stir all ingredients together in a bowl until mixture is sloppy adding a little milk if needed. Put into a greased 1 lb loaf tin.

Cover top of cake mixture with a piece of foil or greaseproof paper to prevent top burning.

Place in a pre-heated oven for 40 – 60 minutes at Gas Mark 4 – a low shelf. Test with skewer to see if cooked.

Slice and serve with butter.

Sweet Cucumber Pickle

"Often called 'bread and butter pickles' in America where this recipe originates. Nice with biscuits and cheese, cold meat or raised pork pie."

3 large cucumbers
2 large onions
2 oz cooking salt

For the syrup:
1 pint distilled malt vinegar
1 lb soft brown sugar
½ level teaspoon each of
ground turmeric and cloves
1 tablespoon whole mustard
seed

Wash the cucumbers, but do not peel. Slice very thinly and place in a mixing bowl in layers with the peeled and sliced onion and salt. Weigh down with a plate and let stand for three hours. After this time the cucumber and onion will be swimming in liquid drawn from the cucumbers. Pour away the salty liquid and thoroughly rinse the vegetables in a colander under running cold water.

Put the vinegar, sugar and spices into a saucepan and stir over low heat to dissolve the sugar. Add the cucumber and onion and bring to the boil. Cook for one minute only – so vegetables remain crisp – then remove from the heat. Using a perforated spoon, scoop out the cucumbers, onion and mustard seed and pack into a suitable container. Replace the saucepan of syrup over the heat and allow to simmer for about 15 minutes to reduce and concentrate the flavour. Pour over the vegetables – there should be enough syrup to cover them. Cool and store.

Elderberry Cough Syrup

4 lbs elderberries
8 pints of water
½ oz of whole cloves
½ oz of whole dried chillies
1 lb of sugar for each pint of juice obtained
Cinnamon sticks

Strip the berries with a fork and boil them in the water, then add cloves and chillies and simmer for 1 hour. Strain through muslin and add 1 lb of sugar to each pint of liquid. Boil again until syrupy.

Bottle with a stick of cinnamon in each bottle. Use a tablespoon in hot water to help clear chesty coughs.

Huntsman's Jelly

2 lb crab apples, washed and roughly chopped
1 lb blackberries
1 lb stripped elderberries
2 pints water
2 lbs granulated sugar (approximately)

Place apples, blackberries and elderberries in a large pan. Add water and simmer gently uncovered for about an hour until the fruit is pulpy. Press with the back of a spoon to mash the fruit.

Strain through a jelly bag or muslin until all the liquid has dripped through. Do not squeeze or try to rush the process as it clouds the jelly. Measure the juice, and to every pint of liquid add 1 lb of sugar.

Dissolve the sugar in juice and boil rapidly for 15 – 20 minutes until jam setting point is reached.

Cranberry Sauce

"I know it is easier to buy this sauce with everything else we all do at Christmas but it is worth that bit of extra effort to make the real thing."

100g of fresh cranberries
4 tablespoons of water
50g of soft brown sugar
2 tablespoons of red wine
2 teaspoons of mixed spice

Place the cranberries in a pan with the sugar, wine and water. Bring to the boil then simmer until the cranberries have popped, and are soft and pulpy. Add the mixed spice and continue to cook for a further 5 minutes.

Bottle and the sauce will keep for up to a 2 months in a refrigerator.

Victoria Fairey   Makes 4 small jars   103

Lemon Curd

"It is really worth the effort"

Grated rind and juice of 4 lemons
4 eggs
100g of butter
450g sugar

Put all the ingredients into the top of a double pan, or a bowl standing in a pan of simmering water.

Stir until the sugar has dissolved, and continue heating and stirring until the curd thickens. Strain (or leave the 'bits' in according to preference) into small prepared and heated jars.

Seal and store in a cool place.

This preserve will only keep for about 1 month, so only make small amounts at a time.

Makes 750g

"On cooling, these biscuits have a soft chewy centre and harden up after a few days. Once made, eat within one week"

2 medium egg whites
225g caster sugar
125g ground almonds
¼ teaspoon almond essence
25 whole blanched almonds

Pre-heat the oven to Gas Mark 4. Whisk the egg whites until stiff. Gradually fold in the sugar, then stir in the almonds and almond essence to form a firm paste.

Spoon teaspoonfuls of the mixture on to baking trays lined with baking parchment, spacing them slightly apart. Press an almond into each and bake for 12-15 minutes until just golden and firm to touch.

Leave to cool. Transfer from the baking trays to wire racks to cool completely. Store in airtight container until required.

Pat Collin

Gorgeous Ginger Flapjacks

8 oz porridge oats
4 oz butter
3 oz soft brown sugar
1 piece of stem ginger
1 tablespoon syrup from jar of stem ginger
3 tablespoons golden syrup

Grease and line an 8" square tin

Chop the ginger very finely.

Place the butter, sugar, and all the syrup in a large saucepan and heat until all the butter melts.
Alternatively, this can also be prepared with a microwave. Stir ingredients together before adding the oats and chopped ginger.

Press into the lined tin and smooth the surface. Bake in the oven at 190°C for 20 minutes, until set and golden brown.

Mark into portions, while still warm, then leave to cool on a wire tray. Remove portions from tray and store in a tin in a cool place.

Spiced Plum Sauce

"This sauce can be used in stir frys, spooned over chicken, pork or sausages 10 minutes before cooking has finished or served with cold meats. It is very easy to do and keeps well in a cool place."

3 lbs soft plums such as 'Victoria', halved and stoned.
½ pint of white wine vinegar
1 lb of soft dark brown sugar
1 dessert spoon of french mustard
2 teaspoons of allspice

Put plums into a large pan and put on a low heat until very, very soft. Cooking time approximately 15 minutes. Add all the other ingredients and heat to boil and simmer for 10 minutes. Take off the stove and allow to cool for 5 minutes. Use an electric hand blender and blend until completely smooth.

Bottle in clean jam-jars, covering immediately.

Victoria Fairey ———————————————— Makes 4 lbs   107

Brenda's Infallible Chocolate Cake

"This recipe will also make 24 small cakes."

8 oz self-raising flour
9 oz caster sugar
½ teaspoon salt
1¼ oz cocoa powder
4½ oz butter or margarine
2 eggs, beaten
6 tablespoons evaporated milk
5 tablespoons warm water
A few drops of vanilla essence

Milk Chocolate Icing:
2½ oz butter or margarine
4 teaspoons cocoa powder
8 oz sieved icing sugar
3 tablespoons milk
1 teaspoon vanilla essence

Sieve together the flour, sugar, salt and cocoa. Rub in the butter or margarine until the mixture resembles breadcrumbs. Beat in the eggs, vanilla essence, water and evaporated milk. Continue to beat until the mixture becomes lighter in colour. Grease and flour two 8" tins and bake in a moderate oven (Gas Mark 4), for 30-35 minutes.

Meanwhile, melt the butter or margarine, blend in the cocoa then sugar, milk and vanilla and beat until smooth. Allow to cool and thicken slightly before using.

When cold, sandwich together and cover with icing.

for Brenda Wright

Pear Chutney

"Make in September and it's perfect for Christmas"

4 lbs pears (when peeled – 5 lbs when whole)
1 lb onions
1 lb tomatoes
1 lb Demerara sugar
8 oz raisins
2 green peppers, deseeded and chopped
Pinch of Cayenne pepper
½ oz salt
1 tablespoon chopped fresh ginger
1½ pint pickling vinegar

Peel, chop and gently simmer the pears, onions and tomatoes for 20 minutes. Add the remaining ingredients to pear mixture and cook gently for 1½ - 2 hours, until a spoon pulled across the surface leaves a furrow.

Pot in clean, warm jam-jars screwing the lids on tightly. Leave to cool and store for at least three months before using.

Kay Lawrance

Apple Flapjacks

1 medium cooking apple
25g sultanas or raisins
90g light muscovado sugar
100g margarine, plus extra for greasing
40g wholemeal self-raising flour
4 oz porridge oats

Preheat the oven to Gas Mark 4. Grease the base and sides of an 18cm round or 15 cm square cake tin with a little margarine. Peel and core the apple and grate into a saucepan. Add the dried fruit, stir in a tablespoon of the sugar and bring to the boil over a medium heat until mixture starts to thicken but is still reasonably moist.

Place the margarine in another pan and heat gently until melted. Remove from heat and stir in the remaining sugar, flour and oats. Spread half of the mixture over the base of the tin, pressing into the edges.

Spoon apple mixture on top, spreading it out evenly. Cover with remaining oat mixture, pressing it down gently and evenly. Bake in the oven for 30-35 minutes until golden brown in colour. Remove from oven and cut when cool.

Zara Kimber ————————————————— Makes 8 slices

Peanut Crisps

"Children enjoy making these"

4 oz soft margarine
4 oz brown sugar
5 oz self raising flour
1 teaspoon instant coffee dissolved in 2
teaspoons hot water
2 oz peanuts

Place all ingredients into mixing bowl. Mix to a soft dough.

Roll into walnut size pieces. Place well apart on a greased baking tray. Flatten slightly with a fork.

Bake 10 – 15 minutes at Gas Mark 4.

Pat Collin

Index

Index

Index

Oven Temperature Conversions

Gas Mark	Degrees F	Degrees C
¼	225	110
½	250	130
1	275	140
2	300	150
3	325	160
4	350	180
5	375	190
6	400	200
7	425	220
8	450	230
9	475	240

Acknowledgements

Thank you to all that helped in the creation of this book, especially the cooks of Ware, both at home and in the food business, who contributed their recipes. A special note of thanks to Jon and Lucy Fairey who, without payment, apart from being fed occasionally, provided all the design and artwork. Without their help this book would not have been possible in its current form. Thank you to the Hanson and West families for proof reading; Rev. Derrick Peel for believing it could be done and encouraging us, and to David Perman for his help in publication and knowledge of Ware History. Our thanks to Ware Town Council and the East Herts District Council Economic Development Unit for their financial support. A thank you also to our printers, Herts & Essex Digital who went that extra mile for us. Editing this book has been a journey, and an adventure for all of us, but we believe the result has been worth the effort. We hope you enjoy it. Be proud of being a Ware cook.

Editors:
Deborah Cock, Victoria Fairey, Kay Lawrance, Ian Little, Joan Peel, Olive Woodhouse

St Mary's Church, Ware

St. Mary the Virgin
High Street
Ware
SG12 9EH

Vicarage ☎01920 464817

Services:
Sunday: 8.00am, 10.00am and
6.30pm
Wednesday 11.00am

We try and keep the church open on
Saturday and Sunday afternoon for
visitors. If you wish to become
involved in caring for this Grade I
listed historic building, why not join
the Friends of St. Mary's. Just pick up

a leaflet at the Ware library or visit www.stmaryware.org.uk. The church can be used for
concerts and events. The modern church hall can be booked for clubs and societies as well as
small family occasions. Please ring the vicarage for details.

And finally.........

"So I commend enjoyment, for there is nothing better for people under the sun than to eat, drink and enjoy themselves, for this will go with them in their toil through the days of life that God gives them under the sun."

Ecclesiastes Chapter 8 verse 15